Girl, Swooning

Girl, Swooning

IMOGEN WADE

corsair poetry

CORSAIR

First published in Great Britain in 2026 by Corsair

1 3 5 7 9 10 8 6 4 2

Copyright © Imogen Wade, 2026

The moral right of the author has been asserted.

*All characters and events in this publication, other than
those clearly in the public domain, are fictitious
and any resemblance to real persons,
living or dead, is purely coincidental.*

All rights reserved.
No part of this publication may be reproduced, stored in a
retrieval system, or transmitted, in any form or by any means, without
the prior permission in writing of the publisher, nor be otherwise circulated
in any form of binding or cover other than that in which it is published
and without a similar condition including this condition being
imposed on the subsequent purchaser.

A CIP catalogue record for this book
is available from the British Library.

ISBN: 978-1-4721-6038-6

Typeset in Garamond by M Rules
Printed and bound in Great Britain by Clays Ltd, Elcograf S.p.A.

Papers used by Corsair are from well-managed forests
and other responsible sources.

Corsair	The authorised representative
An imprint of	in the EEA is
Little, Brown Book Group	Hachette Ireland
Carmelite House	8 Castlecourt Centre
50 Victoria Embankment	Dublin 15, D15 XTP3, Ireland
London EC4Y 0DZ	(email: info@hbgi.ie)

An Hachette UK Company
www.hachette.co.uk

www.littlebrown.co.uk

for Joyce

CONTENTS

Umbilical	1
I Sat with My Grandmother	2
Thirteen	3
Wednesday	4
The Alder Queen	5
Visitor	7
The Time I Was Mugged in New York City	8
Dormitory	9
Meditations on Intimacy	10
Pilates Workout	11
Intergenerational	12
Childhood Crush	13
Himalayas	14
The Perils of Teledentistry	15
Jigsaw	16
Ensoulment	17
Cremation	18
J	19
Encounter	21
Somewhere Near Carn Euny	22
Truro	23
Eunice	24

Camping	25
Same Dream	26
Citizen	27
Fantasy Friend	28
Religious Fervour	29
Girl, Swooning	30
Forms	31
Therapist goes out and meets the devil	32
Tennis Lesson	33
Parable	34
Three Stages of Departure	35
City Blues	36
Not a day goes by that I don't think of you	37
Horror	40
Death Poem for Adults	41
In Stock	42
On a Plane	43
battery	44
Nothing Porn	45
Big Daddy Blue	46
Picnic	48
Snow Child	49
Argos	50
Breakfast	52
Divine Cento	53
Message	54
Women in Art	55
Ferring	56
Bled	58
Desire Poem	59
Waiting Man	60
Do I need another dress?	61

Monologue by Jane Eyre	62
Trip to the Monastery	63
Damsel	64
Sunday Secrets	65
Notes	67
Permissions	69
Acknowledgements	71

'Life is first boredom, then fear'

- Philip Larkin

'Obviously, Doctor, you've never been a thirteen-year-old girl'

- Cecilia Lisbon

Umbilical

I want to devastate you,
think it would do you some good.
The trick is knowing
how your belly button feels—
press inside it
with your nail,
scrape
against
the skin.
You were once connected to your mother,
whoever she was, whoever she is.
You once floated
and didn't use your lungs
to breathe.
Where is she now?
Do you ever
lie in the bath
and try to forget
your name?
There's a reason we call it
waters breaking—
a reason people like to float
face up and pretend
they're minus zero.
Did your mother prefer your potential
to the woman you became?
If she could,
would she take you back inside?
Would you go?

I Sat with My Grandmother

She told me a story
about a pony her family bred
on the farm by Hadrian's Wall,
and how she won a prize
for handling the foal.

One day, her dad found the pony
lying in the Borderlands.
The autopsy found wire
in his stomach—
grey and glinting as rain.

I saw it all: as he was on the day
of the show, soft and ugly,
and at the end, his head baptised
with dew.

She turned her hands
to show me what she held
and I took it from her, without
greed, like folded clothes
to be taken upstairs and put away.

What was the heaviest weight
for my grandmother to carry—
the foal, the wire, or the medal?

Thirteen

You'll learn this about me: I have
no faith in salvation. I keep believing
that a man will punch me in the mouth
although none ever has. I used to get

so angry

as a child, take myself off into a dark
room, get on the floor and bite myself.
Something terrible was always about
to happen— if it didn't, then I'd do it

to myself.

Wednesday

I'm no stranger to doors. I've made my
fair share of entrances. Blood is leaking
down my thighs, but it's not a wound.
Men labour to comprehend. I don't
enjoy generalisations but I will say that
the ocean is water. I used to have perfect
hair that took forever to brush. My irises
are green but their centre is gold. How
like a teenage girl to romanticise her eyes,
to describe her face as if she was the
main character in a book. Sometimes
I forget I'm not a teenager, that I'm almost
a married woman with a mortgage and
responsibilities. Not as many as I could
have, might one day have. It's Wednesday
and there's nothing on my calendar, so
I might drive into the woods again. Call my
mother. Write a book. Wash my hair. Pick
the lint off my mohair jumper. Wash the
blood, see it on my hands and pretend I've
been in a fight. Actually get in a fight. Run
myself a bath. Run laps around the field.
Grow around my grief. Think about all the
magnificent noses that surgeons reduce.
Look at fringe inspiration pictures. Unload
the dishwasher. Pay tax. Go through every
door without a sign. Things like that.

The Alder Queen

I grew up in a haunted house
where, some nights, a woman
visited my room at low light;

she had eyes like blue beetles
and wore a crown of heather
with tall, gleaming feathers.

She measured my skin, told me
it wouldn't do, peeled it off;
I wept, my bones rattled loose.

The Alder Queen never waits
or appeases those who beg,
she said, and grew wings.

We flew over England at night
before the postman's round,
the dog walkers, first light.

She dropped lower and soared
over hedgerows and fields,
until I rolled free on the earth;

then the queen stepped closer,
wrapped me in a velvet robe, and
said *at last you are my creature*.

Some nights, the Alder Queen
slips into my adult dreams,
my heart between her palms;

she eats it in her bed of oak,
as another young girl rests
in the thornbush of her arms.

Visitor

The thing you think happened to you
happened to me too.
One evening, you crouched
on the end of my bed
like a little mouse
and asked me what I knew.
I said: *go away my head is on fire.*
So you crept away,
carrying your parcel of pain,
into the violent night.

The Time I Was Mugged in New York City

I told people that the travel sickness pills
made me stupid. I entered JFK with a red
suitcase and no one to greet me. A man
came up to me, dressed in black. I found
myself in a car park by an expensive van
and he was holding my luggage. *Get in*, he
said. There wasn't a single thought in my
head. I found myself inside his van; he
locked the doors immediately after; made
me switch my phone off as we went under
the bridge. We spoke about Niagara Falls.
He chose the narrowest roads in the city,
a needle making a joke out of Manhattan.
When he pulled up outside Grand Central
station, he said—*don't get out, there are
bad people around*. He made me unzip
my suitcase, books and bras spilling over
the seat, and give him all my money. Then
he helped me out of the van like I was a
princess; he held my bags like a vassal and
kissed my cheek. *Get in*, I hear whenever
a man pushes me too far; get into my big
black car. Sometimes in my dreams, I am
sitting beside him on the leather; I don't
need to be ordered and together, we drive
with melodious speed over the East River.

Dormitory

I had a room to myself like
all the exchange students—
the college knew the Europeans
would revolt if they had to bunk
like freshmen. I had two beds
in my room, one never made up.
I covered the floor with clothes
over and over. One humid night,
I'm asleep when someone tries to
break my door down. Slamming
their fists. Throwing their full
weight against it. I wake and lie
like a shifty fox in the darkness,
watching the wooden door in
the dormitory shake. The person
is shouting; if it's not my name,
it's something very like it. I wait
to be seized, chased by thrill;
the same one I get when I'm on
the motorway and nearing the
scene of a crash. I don't want
accidents to happen but if they
have to, then at least let me look.
Someone is smashing my door,
moonlight on the carpet, but the
lock holds. It goes on for so long
that I become frustrated. I think:
show me the blood, show me
the wrecked metal. Come in.

Meditations on Intimacy

I admit it's a surprise to see you here.
I thought the robin may have taken you
but your lungs are still wheezing.

I used to walk down by the river.
For all I know, you were one of the men I passed
in the blackest December.

Years fell forward like drunk girls
on pavements;
we didn't catch a single one.

Commonality is a form of intimacy,
like being born in the same hospital or loving
Brie. I feel closer to you than ever before.

At opposite ends of a long dining table,
the kind you see in stately homes, we shared
our time apart like a meal.

Pilates Workout

The carpet is soft under my back.
I am slick as a Calippo ice lolly.
Lower my spine; exhale to bridge;
back down. What advice would I
give myself if I was not myself?
I used to love nothing better than
being wrong. Babies are born all
the time; not a single one is mine.
I practise contralateral twists with
breath control, thoracic rotations,
pelvic tilts, spinal flexion. Sunday's
workout will be chest flys, narrow
squats, bicep curls. The final goal
is to raise my grief over my head
like a hundred kilogram kettlebell.

Intergenerational

My grandmother grew up on rations
and ate that way forevermore, though
food was the centre of my mother's
house and I grew up full. Now hunger
and satiation wrestle in my gullet,
like twins that swallow each other.
In my father's house I cut turmeric for
the curry and stained my fingers; my skin
is a lesson in loyalty, though I've scoured
my hands raw. I like apples—poison or
not, they clean my teeth and I've heard
that everything will kill you if you eat
it all. I'd like to take the time to thank
my fictional husband and fictional children,
who never argue; who pass the salt;
who never wage, between servings, war.

Childhood Crush

Surely you understand
what you meant to me—
your uncatalogued vastness,
leather shoes on the tiles,
your lighthouse smile?
I remember my stiff jaw,
the hot shame in my throat
that I was unable to respond
in kind, for my eyes
were already on the evening.
You called me a word,
struck me with it like a bell,
and turned my skin transparent.

Himalayas

An English woman in a care home
told me that she'd married a man from
the Himalayas when she was young.
He died before her and she went back
to the mountains and left his ashes
on the ground. This story moved me
absurdly—in my mind's eye, I watched
a woman with strong thighs and a plait
over one shoulder climb a mountain,
wind stinging her face until her tears
evaporated into the air. In the present,
her eyes held mine: so black and so full.
I could smell the rocks. I could taste
her grief. And the years were stacked
like piles of cash in a heist movie—
the years between him and her;
the years between her and me.

The Perils of Teledentistry

'Look not on his countenance . . .'

- 1 Samuel 16:7

It's been many years & we haven't been together
for any of them. But you're really helping me out.

I bought aligners online & they gave me bone loss
(permanent) above my teeth. You hate that I did
this to myself & never understood my need to fix.

I dieted, tried to be as skinny as a crescent moon.
I dyed my hair ash blonde & donated my clothes.

We're walking down a path through Painshill Park.
I tell you about my wobbly teeth. They're straight
but also they could go black & fall out at any time.

You don't say anything for a while. We slouch into
the crystal grotto & you murmur into the purple—

> *I think you're beautiful
> & I've always wanted to tell you.*

Your voice is deep. You've only ever complimented
women you're sleeping with or related to. I bump
my shoulder against yours like nothing's changed.

It sounds like you look at me with the Lord's gaze.
If I'd known, would I still be able to eat an apple?

Jigsaw

I have seen angels
in my life: gnarled,
garbed, crimson angels

and where life is,
Death is not; where
Death is, life is not

I wonder if I've
created the gods
that haunt me

they stood by our cribs
in ugly pageantry,
blurred as a post-meds
delusion

where is the blanket
to keep me warm,
is it on
the highest shelf?

they chase me
in the valley's cut,
playing the world's
oldest game

if I had any passion left

I would pour it

down your throat

my whole life
I have been on my
tippy toes

I long to belong
to one of
them completely

will we catch her,
or will her spirit
outrun us?

and where life goes,
Death goes

without this
adulterous longing

I can claim
intimacy with both

Ensoulment

for Charlotte

Before my head crested,
I loved you. Since our
conception, I learned to
live around you, two
chestnuts squished close
in one case. You were the
one I knew, before we
met the one who fed us.
I went first into the cold air;
entered to a soundtrack
of strangers, you to your
womb-mate's cry—
was that your sacrifice,
chasing me into the light?

Cremation

I have an image of what will happen
in a few days: the coffin ablaze. Then
there will be no feet for the shoes,
no legs for the trousers, no waist for
the belt, and no wrists for the bangles.

J

I'm holding her hand but I know she's
not really with me. She's in the stables
of the soul, polishing her riding boots.
She reaches for a saddle on the rack—
she brushes flakes of mud and coughs
from the dust. Her chestnut mare makes
little sounds; she knows that the horse
is restless, hungering for the afternoon.
She's not sure why she's twenty again:
she could swear she'd been somewhere
else, doing something important. Her
arms are corded with a rider's muscle
and her back is erect as a marionette's.
She whispers her horse's name, which
she'd almost forgotten—but surely not,
she was here just yesterday. The smell
of hay and boot polish is a thick woollen
embrace. She woke up this morning
in her bed in the farmhouse and spoke
to her parents over tea; she's never held
a baby before, she's never gone North.
There's nobody in the stables or in the
fields, but there are horses, and she's
always preferred them anyway. She has
some time left before she has to ride—
she feels like she's waiting for a signal.
It will be the carnyx's call; she thinks she
dreamt this last night. She will recognise
the sound, even though she has never
heard the sound. The cold sun grazes

the tops of the corn. Birds chirp in the
trees; she hasn't yet learned their names,
and has never known pain. Her horse
sighs again. Soon, she says, soon.

Encounter

I dream of my grandmother
walking backwards down the stairs,
my hands around her wrists to keep
her from falling. She asks me
where her husband is; I say he is dead.
*Then why do his books and clothes
still fill the rooms?* I ask her
how old she is. *I'm in my forties.*
I shake my head. *Then, twenties.*
I am her granddaughter
but in her logic we can be the same age
at the same time. The year is 1959.
We keep walking down the stairs,
and they are endless.

Somewhere Near Carn Euny

This landscape will kill you if you let it
but what happens is: you survive and find
that a lack of mercy isn't what kills you.
When you don't let a deathly thing kill you,
you realise that you're strong. There is
nothing finer than this. You will cast off the
life you knew and swap it for a surname
hewn from rock. Lichen in summer under
your hands; umber hills; flowering gorse.
There is only one choice: death or change.

Truro

Last week's wildfire burned the woods;
through the rain, I can see the absence.
Pillars of smoke bulldozed for days, like
a Doomsday cult's gates to the next life.

We killed the lights at bedtime and kept
the windows thrown open in the heatwave
to scout the breeze—instead, our room
held the sound of fire hoses on the hills.

Above the city is a new planet where
nothing grows, its borders demarcated
by singed gold. Surviving pine trees loom
like Stonehenge sarsens around an altar.

Or like a fairy circle, which is a prettier
notion, and reminds me of the old stories
of my country. But when I step inside
there is no other world, or other self.

Eunice

The monstrous wind begins its task
of shaking down the trees. My lungs
feel full. Not of disease, but ghosts—
I can't breathe the way I used to.
There's a red warning for this storm.
It makes it so easy to believe in God.

Camping

We sit here and I love you like a harvest,
I love you like a well-built house, I love you
like a birthday cake, I love you like a river.
We go up and down together, we light up,
we feed on each other, we live inside love
like this tent we have put up in heavy rain.
There haven't been any storms this month,
mostly showers, but the tent is made of nylon
so the water can't get through. Sometimes
I feel like I'm drowning but it's just thick air
in the muggy evening, with fluttering moths
against the solar lamp. Your face is tanned
and there are lines around your open eyes.
I'm stirring baked beans on the Trangia.
I love you like a grey evening walking back
from the station, when clouds are streaks,
when the gulls are quiet, the roads empty,
and there's light in the window at home.

Same Dream

Every night before I go to sleep,
I walk through two fields of rape.
Silver truck; smell of weed; soft
flannel of your shirt; kitchen light
and no one else but you for miles:
it's waiting for me over the trees.
You're stirring soup on the stove,
I know you are, though I'm still in
the fields. I tread the same dried
mud on repeat and when I'm not
asleep, I ache for flowering rape.
The dream is a net that I slip into
every night like a minnow.

Citizen

I filled myself with the catch of the day,
mother-baked bread, English blackberries;
trailed the hem of my dress through all the
parishes of this country—summer, long
grass. *Once upon a time* is how we do it;
Armenians say *it both was and was not*.
Once upon a time, when it both was and
was not, a woman awoke in a grey barrow
knowing only herself, life as relevant to her
as the moon to a captive goldfish. I open
my arms to the body and the spark, but
that's too simple. The final line is—
there's no sign that points towards home.
(So do we spend all our days adrift,
wandering, wondering, desert-bereft?
I am quite sure that words run out when
the sand starts. Will I find love in the dunes?
Will I eat the stars for breakfast? How big
is a whale? How white will our vertebrae
bleach under Australia's sun?) No guide, no
demarcated way, just heat that twists our
organs; heat that drowns us and we let it.
I was a butterfly before I was a caterpillar.
Life is a series of was and was nots. God is
very tired from bearing you on His back.

Fantasy Friend

You never do anything bad—
which surprises me,
because in the space of my dream
you'd never be held accountable.
Men don't go to jail for things they do
in women's dreams. But you're
a safe man, a good man.
I dream of being a child crouching down
in the grounds of my old school.
There are men in army gear swarming
and big Alsatians sniffing me.
You come over, say into a headset:
I'm helping a friend, then reach out a hand
and raise me up.

Religious Fervour

The afternoon
licks my thighs
and, somewhere
in another life, He
pins me to the bed.
His voice enters—
I've always wanted
to see you come
undone like this.

Girl, Swooning

At my wedding dress fitting, I almost
fainted in the shop. They stripped it off.
I sat in the changing room in a thong and heels,
sweat between my breasts like an ice cube
dancing on a warm surface. Philippa held
a cold compress to the back of my neck.
Maureen fanned paper like a palm leaf and Sheila
cut me a banana. I was beautiful, I thought,
once I could lift my head from between my knees—
in the freestanding gilt mirror, my face pale like a
storybook and my hair like Nausicaa's. But by
then I was bare, clammy and loose. It felt
feminine to swoon in a bridal shop, like I'd ascended
to womanhood. Sheila said brides had fainted
before, it wasn't uncommon. Yes, I have
joined their ranks—all those smiling dolls
propped on plush carpet, framed by wreaths and veils.
Before I went down, stuck with pins, my chest
like starless space, I said: *am I supposed to recognise myself?*

Forms

Barbara Hepworth Exhibition, Tate St Ives, 2023

i

do you recall the white sphere
that prayed to the cross

& the form locked away
that sang through the case
& begged to be touched?

ii

it 'moved' me. buzz
began in my grey matter
& slid the slow slip of art
down my spine; love like a ride, a
kind of prayer. a kind of god/mother
holding child or mother holding mother.

iii

I wanted to pluck the strings
& run oil over the wood; would feel,
I believed, like kissing the moon.
or would it feel like my heart,
stripped down to the artery
& the rush of my desires?

Therapist goes out and meets the devil

I dream of a castle, a turret, an angel's indifferent counsel.
He tells me:

> *Foxes have their dens and birds have their nests,*
> *but humans have no place to lie down and rest*

then takes me to bed. There are wax pears in dishes on the
sideboard; a decanter, a wall of windows, dancing candles.
His lips are cherries soaked in vodka.

He plants seeds inside me, but not the kind that make a child.
They're taking root—mustard or embers, I can't tell.
He says:

> *You will reap fire or else a field.*

Tennis Lesson

In the dream you head right, through the arch into the empty park. They said the floodlights would mark your way but the tennis courts are dark. You've only been here in the day. Tomorrow, you will say you misread the flyer; tonight, you are a girl who's joined a tennis club that doesn't exist. From around the bend, on the concrete path, come footsteps (a man—who else would walk through darkness so casually?). Nerves raw as a blister, you ease the strap over your head and place your bag on the ground; you step out of your trainers and stand in your socks. You run, noiseless as a bird's wings. You're certain now your survival instinct works; you do want to live. This is an interesting fact to be examined later, better than any tennis lesson. He may have wanted to examine night-blooming flowers or, stifled, to breathe fresh air. It doesn't matter why he was there. This nightmare has taught you to always be grateful for fear.

Parable

In the oldest country of them all,
a narrow stream runs over rocks.
There are no birds on the banks
or laundresses scrubbing shirts,
just water from the world's eyes.

The stream follows the staircase
of the mountainside: under stars,
through mossy woods, past men
who raise cups of water for the
priests to bless. Only one drinks.

The stream follows the staircase
of his body—from lips to soul,
a lifetime's worth of movement.
The other men pour sacred water
onto their fallow fields and hope.

Judgement comes to the village
and He tips the men's souls into
His hands. Only one is polished
smooth as glass—the man who
drank and whose family starved.

Three Stages of Departure

When I thought about your death,
I imagined you leaving. I knew that
one day I would get the call to say
your taxi was outside, and wave as
you carried your bag down the drive.
I never imagined you taking down
paintings, polishing off perishables,
and paying for your own cremation.
I didn't expect the Bechstein to move,
to see its imprint on the green carpet.
I'm surrounded by sellotaped boxes
and strangers disassembling your life.
What comes after the preparation?
You going away, which I've imagined;
then you staying gone, which I haven't.

City Blues

I'm wearing a long dress again,
patterned like a curtain. It brushes
against the escalator in the station,
and I remember what it was like
to wake up in places so silent that
I heard mist settle on the grass.
It's better to be with others, even
if no one knows my name. I take
up space on a stool, in a cubicle,
or when my hand grasps the rail.
It took me five years to learn that
hills can't bear witness; to become
real, I had to leave the cairns I love.

Not a day goes by that I don't think of you

I want to get a Doberman
that I will walk every day
into the woods. I will let my thoughts
of you be swallowed by
his paws eating up ground.

I've lost things I don't want back.
Be a star, whatever, be ash on the wind:
stay gone, I won't disturb
what's already passed through.
You spoke a lot
about the ephemeral.
These bodies can't catch what we are,
they are sieves
and we slip through their nets.

We're done.
There's always more to say
but no mouth to say it with.
I've got mine,
yours was put in an oven.

The Doberman I don't have
barks at a stranger through the trees.
He loves me, that attachment
we call love, we don't know what else
to call it.

I think of Argos keeping vigil on Ithaca
against all odds;

like my Doberman, a dog
from a poem.
They do justice to the way we love, love
that called me to your bedside
in a hospital room
that smelled of the First Noble Truth.
I remember
the set of your face,
your arms. Bearing witness,
I felt like Argos:
fulfilling the possible, impossible
destiny of his faith.

I was born loyal. Born loving.
Born intractable. And,
like Odysseus beholding Argos,
I dashed a tear from my face,
knowing I could not
tell the world what you were to me.

A father who wasn't my father, a poet
who never wrote a line.
As we lay in a heap of manure
buzzing with flies,
both of us dogs,
you were again the mystic
who taught me how to dream.

Once you frowned at me
across the dining room table;
when I asked what you were thinking,
you said: *I will never*

know what you'll look like
middle-aged. I'm
trying to picture it.
I thought it was mere curiosity;
all faces change shape.
I watched your cheeks sink.

But it was the dog in you
needing to know,
wanting to wait.

Horror

I imagine what my jewellery will look like
a hundred years from now, when I'm not around
to wear it. Too cheap to pass down. Landfill?
Grave? Just gone—the way gold plating disappears?
The butterfly earrings; the locket; the fake pearls.
Lost things all live somewhere. Tarnished
bracelet without a wrist; soil-encrusted ring
without a finger; my baubles floating in water.

Death Poem for Adults

Death brushed dust from the sleeves of his coat. He arched a plucked eyebrow when I started to screech, then delivered a speech made of vellum and ink.

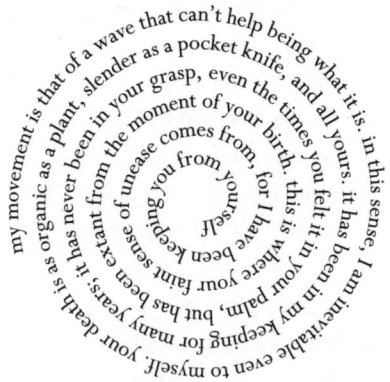

His words are an exam question I want to pass. I think of how death is 'a fact of life' and also how it is the opposite of life. Some people see it as a mercy; others see it as a threat. After meeting Death last night, I see my life as the closest Death can get to love—my days so far have gone unchecked.

In Stock

Whenever I feel this way, I also feel afraid,
like seeing flashing lights in my rearview;
I'm ready to pull over to let the sirens pass,
but it's just an ordinary car. False alarm.
I'm having bad dreams again, waking with
a seasick stomach. If I bought the perfect
dress, would my problems disappear?
Everyone who likes clothes has believed
this at least once. Instead of meditating,
I picture a dress of yellow cotton, with puff
sleeves and a faux wrap tie. It's made by
hand but not by mine. There isn't a lining
and the fabric turns slightly sheer when
I stand in tall grass, lit by the sun; enough
to see the outline of my legs, the suggestion
of my breasts. I walk through the grass,
towards who knows where, thinking who
knows what. This is how I relax before bed.
I'd spend my savings on the perfect dress.

On a Plane

I find myself on a plane above
a mountain range. Grey, streaked
with white. Towns in the cracks.
My brain offers me thoughts on a
platter as if serving me dinner—
isn't your suicide inevitable, isn't
the choice of nothing better than
what could eat you up tomorrow?
The mountains become forests—
the kind we killed off in England;
I want to rest on their green quilts.
The forests become a city. An hour
ago over the sea, there was a wind
farm of tiny white hands, waving
like children from train windows.
We lose height. The terminal leers
closer and closer. My heart is with
the turbines on the water. Then
we bump tarmac and suicide is as
distant as my dream of climbing the
mountains—something that other
people do. Maybe I shouldn't have
read a book about prisoners on a
haunted island. Maybe tomorrow
will be better. Maybe today will.

battery

moon   sky   ground   and   tomb

+

sickening   and didn't I waste my peace when the   following
night kidnapped me on a current of stars

a   each

of   other

−

phases   and didn't I miss the summers when I   my
slept through the blooming of the flowers

like   life   adult   whole

Nothing Porn

My mum's friend came back from a holiday
with a rare Greek illness. Maybe you've got
a rare Greek illness too, she said. I was home
for the summer and couldn't lift my arms up
above my head, could barely leave the bed.
It was the summer I wrote a porn script and
emailed it to Serbia (they sent me headshots
of women and asked me to pick one to star);
the same summer that I found God in a glass,
cancelled the show, blamed porn on Greece.
It was the summer I was a stuttering corpse;
the summer I flew to Kraków and watched
fake buildings collapse like a house of cards.
It was the summer she took me to the GP
and it was the first summer I begged a man
to save me, in a doctor's office in a town
that wasn't my hometown or my real town
but my mother's town, where a rare Greek
illness was on the loose. She picked me up
from the local surgery and said, anything?
But nothing, it was the summer of nothing.

Big Daddy Blue

' for that dark companion
stays on your heels . . .'

- Horace, *Satires* (2.7)

We bumped into each other on Oxford Street.
First sight of him in four years, I was scared
to death. *Girly whirly*, he said, *I want to fry*
you like an egg for lunch. Yum yum yum.

I stepped back but he grabbed my waist,
his palms hot as a geothermal rock, and
dried my veins; he was July sunshine and
I was on a washing line, a pair of socks.

I got away but met him on the Tube the next
day; he kissed me and I wished he tasted
of mould to remind me he was a disease—
instead, daisy chains wound round my
tongue and he called me summer's queen.

In the office, he didn't speak to me once
but lurked by the water cooler and shot
smirks my way. I changed tactics, let him
walk me home from work without a fight.

He stormed inside, knew which door was
mine, and shut me in the oven of his body—
like being locked in a car in a heatwave, like
drought or thirst or love without resolution.

I won't eat you after all, he said, *I'd lose my
best opponent*. He made no move to leave;
kept me wrapped in the moment. *Or maybe
I will*, he mumbled into my shoulder, his last
words before we fell asleep. *But not tonight*.

Picnic

I'm eating fruit in the woods. Black pine trees.
Low tide. Canada geese in a V overhead—
maybe going home.

This peach is sweet. Everybody and their mum
likes eating peaches. Am I too abrasive? Am I
peach enough?

I'm sucking flesh from the stone, sweetness
clinging to the edge. I imagine the stone
is really a well.

I make a wish and throw a penny in because
getting what I want is a tall tale: this one secret,
impossible thing.

If the peach was kind, she would return the coin
as evidence that unmet desire
has no consequence.

But this is an honest well, so my palm stays empty,
and the coin I kissed before I threw it
is still falling.

Snow Child

I remember you with spots on your chin
as you packed snow into your hands
and pressed a smiley face against the wall
in your mother's driveway. You were
wearing the black duffel coat she bought
you for Christmas. You said *you don't
need to be special when staying alive
is the mission* and some days I repeat
that like a mantra. No one else's wisdom
outdoes yours. Snow child: when rain
punches my roof at night and I wake up
scared to be alone, for a moment it's
like I never left that quiet street.
I move my palm over the white sheet,
but really I'm standing in the driveway
with you once more, cupping snow.

Argos

I'm dreaming of getting a Doberman again.
My landlord would say no, even though I haven't asked
and never will. So I don't know. But I dream of Argos
clawing at my door. Dream of him tearing my silk dresses.
Dream of his black eyes by the side of my bed,
begging me for the hills.
I first started dreaming of Argos when we scattered ashes
over gorse on Harting Down. Wind came and fine dust
rose like smoke from the bush, à la Exodus.
Once upon a time, a man with a heart and a liver
and a shiny black hat used to sit on the hill – he watched
over the village, could see the church steeple
and our roof. Man became ash. Then my love became
grief became a Doberman, a dog called Argos
filled with faith. He needs over two hours of exercise daily
and his stamina is the stuff of myth. He has good recall,
so his name is a leash. I tell my mother to count
her blessings, I could have worse coping mechanisms
than taking my fictional Doberman for a walk.
Argos is an island in my aloneness, made of loyalty
and a glossy black coat. The sunlight loves him.
Sometimes I can't get rid of the sight of the yellow petals
turning grey as we tipped his remains –
the way we hid their colour, and sometimes I cry.
Argos licks my face. I feed him a treat. I lie on my back
in the grass; I hear him panting beside me.
Argos who is grief who is love can seem indefatigable,
which is why his breed is known for full body slams
and growls that could make an army plead defeat.
I run him ragged, let him work out the power in his heavy

muscles. Then he sits on my lap in the evening like he doesn't know his own weight.

Breakfast

My chair is the colour
of an aubergine's soft flesh.
I lean on the table, its legs
supported by a cardboard wedge.
A robin pecks seeds on the deck
and this is a long time ago
and you are long dead.

Divine Cento

Lit up[1] like pillars of smoke[2]
against the terrors of the night,[2]
my sleeves stay soaked in darkness.[3]

Wild with spring,[4]
I will climb the palm tree;
I will grasp its branches[2]
and coming upon the fruit,
find it green.[5]

Break both my arms
and I will hold you fast.[5]
As soon as it grows light,
it grows dark.[3]

Even the crickets
who don't know our world at all
cry:[3]

*I was almost falling asleep
when I felt your touch.*[1]

---

1 *Gilgamesh*, trans. Stephen Mitchell
2 *Song of Songs*, Amplified Bible
3 Izumi Shikibu, trans. Jane Hirshfield
4 Ono No Komachi, trans. Jane Hirshfield
5 Rilke, trans. Ranson and Sutherland

Message

Sometimes we are insects,
communicating with each other
from opposite ends
of a vast yellow field—
rubbing our wings, tapping our feet,
vibrating in the air.
I picture us as tiny creatures
rummaging in the tall grass. I know
that there's someone out there
of my kind,
though it has been many years
and our acquaintance will never be
renewed. Yet you are still
in my life—faith without sight,
love without words.

Women in Art

The Rossettis Exhibition, Tate Britain, 2023

I coveted Proserpine's dark interiority
and turned from the Beloved in her overt
perfection—knew, even then, that mystery
was the goal: self-containment, clutching
my pomegranate, unable to be known.
My favourite was *The Annunciation*, with
Christina dyed red. Even in the presence
of the herald and shadowed by a god
who had colonised her womb, the heroine
took without giving—her thoughts were
her own, unable to be entered. It would take
a strange man (in fact, not a man at all)
to hunger for Mary's white and rumpled bed.

Ferring

The world touched me, it
wanted me, needed to enter me
and possess me the way girls
get their bodies thrown around
by demons in horror films—
yes, like breath, like blood, I was
filled up by the world and today
it was the sea, dirty as a sewer
on a cold English day, gulls
bobbing on the waves like dust
particles on boxing gloves.

Fireworks went off last night
behind the blinds, and I cried
for want of seeing them. In the
morning, I drove us to the sea—
it was imperative, my whole
body was burning, and if I hadn't
gone to the coast a part of
me would have died. I was
sliding off life, melting cartilage
on the spinal ridge, and only
beauty could resurrect me.

It's the New Year, a time for
Apollo's archaic torso and also
home truths, such as: the tastiest
thing in the world that will kill
you is a man's honest desire.
I ask everyone for truth and

nobody's ever asked for it back
apart from him. I wish prettiness
mattered less. I wish I didn't
feel ashamed. Words are houses
and he sits in what I've made.

I drove down Long Furlong,
where he'd travelled when he
was growing up—what a quirk of
love, that I care about who
he was before I knew him.
He asked about my resolutions;
I told him that the fireworks made
me cry because they sounded
like everything I've ever wanted.
I want to paint my nails green
and light a fuse and never die.

Bled

I used to avoid water
because it meant nudity—
think of all the water
I never knew; never felt
heavy against my legs,
or soft on the underside
of my arms. Now what?
A turquoise becoming,
a cobalt birth into the
summer lake.

Desire Poem

I joined our hands together, sparrow-light—
whined and kneeled and would not shrink—
climbed the Beacon and died at the top—
I would never see the world like that again—
felt like Laertes's shroud—made then unfurled—
a type of devotion—can confirm that it hurt—
your hands tried to press me whole—as the wind
shook out my hair and clothes—clay unformed—
fabric unstitched—the airy days—the summer
tomb—every book unread—each November
a cloudy cliff we never jumped—off—Atlantic
blues—so far from the house—tucked away
in the Old Town—where I learnt to speak
pieces of sea glass, round-edged, ejaculating
eroded pleasure—the stile, cross-legged, waiting
for Jane—comes evening in the glade, ever true—
and have I been waiting my whole long life
for a watered apple tree—for the fruit?

Waiting Man

In my secret of secrets, you are waiting for me
with the face you wear when you're feeling something
that looks like you're feeling nothing. You're standing
in a swathe of empty land without birdsong or seasons.
You tuck hair behind your ear and get out your cross. But
in real life, I never saw you pray, not once. Did you ever
go to church and sit in the pew with your ankles crossed?
I feel hot all over. I feel like overripe fruit. Mushy black
bananas make the best cake, or so I've heard. My arms
and legs want to move—push ups, squats, run—my body
wants to work at something other than loving you. Tea
in the morning tastes like it's already afternoon. And in my
secret of secrets, you're there. Waiting. As if you know
all my questions. As if you're ready to throw away the
answers. Butterflies thirst for your knuckles and England
misses you, but you chose emptiness instead: this land
without scars or summer. If only you knew that my skin
is yours already; it's waiting for you the way you're waiting
for me and it needs you like the butterflies do. Foam stalks
the tide; I cut myself on crescent moons; the countryside
misses your boots. Just tell me: if I let your emptiness
seep into me, would you let my love sink into you?

Do I need another dress?

*'The Unconscious [...] was for Nerine
  a gigantic subterranean wardrobe.'*

      - Eva Ibbotson, *Magic Flutes*

I dream of wearing a dress
that I wanted to buy several years ago
and never did. Floral, fitted, with a buttoned front
and ruffled straps that fall
off my shoulders. Hem below my knees.
I dream of walking through a dark church in
a rural village in France, faded medieval frescoes
on the walls. Flames lit
by the grieving living for the beloved dead.
I'm wearing a cropped jacket
and a black shoulder bag my grandmother
had in her wardrobe when she died.
My lips are painted. I look like a woman,
if you close your eyes and imagine
a grown-up, sophisticated woman who travels
on her own to European art galleries,
I am that woman.

Monologue by Jane Eyre

He goes to me—*I like being the boss, I tell someone*
to do something and they hop right to it. So I smile
full wide and not a very submissive smile either.
He tells me I haven't lived yet but his eyes are glinting,
as if experience is one of the treats he has in store for me.
We hook up and then lightning splits the trunk (it was
on the news). He tells me he wants to chain me up.
He keeps dropping hints that he's got secrets, but
show me a man who hasn't. Still, this one's pretty bad;
all things considered, a definite red flag. He cares for
his ex with a private nurse and a whole flat to herself—
the red flag is he never told me. I could have helped.
He tries to steal happiness and ignores the conditions.
I will make myself scarce but before I do, he offers to
set us up in a villa in the Mediterranean. I picture wine,
sea, and going at it like rabbits all day long. He tells me
he's thought about raping me and even killing me, but
it's not really my body he wants. He wants what's inside.
I should be scared and I am, I'm not dumb enough to
stick around, but there's an odd romance to his speech.
What he wants from me isn't something he can take.

Trip to the Monastery

He stops at the newsagents for a smoke,
lights it in the car and solemnly inhales
by the back door of the Chinese takeaway,
then throws the rest away. *I only wanted one.*

The dirt track wavers in pebbled darkness;
we lean over the handbrake to touch lips.
He coaxes forgiveness from my tongue,
the catch releases. I am soft again.

We wait in the shrine room for the bell.
I gesture slowly, like I'm moving my arms
through maple syrup. He folds himself up
to masquerade as a chanting monk.

I have a vision of my lover in black robes,
reheating soup, hunched over the stove.
I'm swimming in the air until the gear shift
resurrects my awareness with motion.

We eat leftovers when we get home,
takeaway noodles with black bean sauce.
He smiles at me and I stroke his brown curls.
Our future gleams at the edges of my vision.

We sit together under the humming lights
of the late-night kitchen. I feel like I'm looking
at him through rain; he's thinner than ever.
I've never seen an old man look so young.

Damsel

A teenager almost drowned in the Thames.
I jumped off London Bridge and somehow
got her to shore. I was interviewed for the
papers; my mum has the page on her wall.
A month later, I rescued a hijacked plane,
but soon enough the daydreams changed
when I gave myself permission to be saved.
Across hot coals, through nettles, and into
the sugary mouth of the leopard—he came,
the man I was falling for, elegant and in no
rush. It's how I knew I loved. On death row,
over a volcano, into mist, I'm far from lost.
I don't feel fear. If the lights went out, I know
he would carry me through the dark forever.

Sunday Secrets

My own life feels like honey. I have been transported
here strangely and randomly, to lie on a cream
leather sofa whilst he prepares a meal. After my recent
depression, I still don't like white skies;
claustrophobic when I can't see a slice of blue skin.
I also don't like lies—they're a veil, to obfuscate
the nerves of our bodies. It's not that I'm sensitive,
just aware of how many pores there are in my arms
when I hold them out in the rain. This is how I know
I'm human, though I've doubted it; when rabbits bow
through the Merry Maidens, it is ordinary ground to them.
When clouds tip their hair across Tresillian River, a woman
rinsing her head under a tap, life feels like a secret
I have with him—as if we are the only people left alive
who understand beauty. The heat of the oven reaches me
on the sofa; I don't know what he's making, I trust it
will be good. Memories rise like goosebumps
and I know that a part of me will always be cold—
I've made my peace with it, woven my pain in gold thread
and called it a tapestry. I close my eyes; think of rabbits
on the moors and worry that I haven't given them enough
credit. I don't know what it's like to live as a rabbit,
communing with others in a dawn clearing—maybe in
another life. But I don't want to leave this one, even when
I do. I have a new motto to keep me here, considering
the mystical potential of small mammals. When the sky dips
like a stock chart in the red and my sister sends me a text,
I'll tell you the truth: there's too much beauty to quit.

NOTES

'The Alder Queen' is a gender-reversed folklore retelling of the Erlking, a figure known by different names across European folklore. A version of him features in *Der Erlkönig* by Goethe.

'J' refers to a carnyx, a Celtic wind instrument used in Iron Age Europe. I was inspired by the work of musician and craftsman Samuel Meric.

'Big Daddy Blue' quotes Horace's *Satires* 2.7.115, a line which may have inspired the black dog metaphor for depression. My poem was written to the soundtrack of 'Daddy Blue' by Brad stank.

'Therapist goes out and meets the devil' paraphrases Matthew 8:20 and Luke 9:58. The poem references the Parable of the Mustard Seed.

'Not a day goes by that I don't think of you' and 'Argos' reference Book 17 of *The Odyssey*, in which Odysseus and his dog Argos see each other for the first time in twenty years.

'Monologue by Jane Eyre' paraphrases several lines from Charlotte Brontë's novel, especially from Chapter 27.

'Sunday Secrets' is the name of the PostSecret blog, a community arts project that involves people anonymously sharing secrets by postcard. 'There's too much beauty to quit' appeared as a secret in February 2023.

PERMISSIONS

'Dockery and Son', *The Whitsun Weddings*, copyright © Estate of Philip Larkin. Used by permission of Faber & Faber Ltd.

The Virgin Suicides, copyright © 1993 by Jeffrey Eugenides. Used by permission of HarperCollins Publishers Ltd.

Gilgamesh, translation copyright © 2004, 2005 by Stephen Mitchell. Used by permission of Profile Books Ltd.

Song of Songs 3:6; 3:8; 7:8, the Amplified Bible, copyright © 2015 by The Lockman Foundation.

'It seems a time has come', 'They say winter days', 'If I lived' and 'My body, wandering, lost' from *The Ink Dark Moon: Love Poems by Ono No Komachi and Izumi Shikibu, Women of the Ancient Court of Japan*, translated by Jane Hirshfield with Mariko Aratani, translation copyright © 1986, 1987, 1988, 1989, 1990 by Jane Hirshfield. Used by permission of Vintage Books, an imprint of the Knopf Doubleday Publishing Group, a division of Penguin Random House LLC. All rights reserved.

The Book of Hours, Rainer Maria Rilke, *Selected Poems*, translation copyright © 2011 by Susan Ranson and Marielle Sutherland. Used by permission of Oxford University Press through PLSclear.

Magic Flutes by Eva Ibbotson, first published in 1982 by Century, and in 2009 by Pan, an imprint of Pan Macmillan, a division of Macmillan Publishers International Limited. Reproduced by permission of Macmillan Publishers International Limited. Copyright © Eva Ibbotson 1982, 2009.

ACKNOWLEDGEMENTS

Poems in this book originally appeared in the following places: *The London Magazine*, *PN Review*, *Amsterdam Quarterly*, *The Poetry Review*, *Basket Magazine*, *PERVERSE*, *The Ekphrastic Review*, *Bi+ Lines: An Anthology of Contemporary Bi+ Poets*, the National Poetry Competition, the Ware Poetry Competition, the Winchester Poetry Competition, the Plough Poetry Prize, *The Moth* Poetry Prize, the Wells Festival of Literature Poetry Competition, and the Montreal International Poetry Competition.

Thank you to The Poetry Society for inspiring me when I was a young poet. Thank you to Jenny Hewson, my agent at Lutyens & Rubinstein, and Sarah Castleton, commissioning editor at Corsair, for believing in this book. Thank you to Martha Sprackland, copy-editor, and my friend Naomi for editing the manuscript.

Girl, Swooning is dedicated to my grandmother Joyce (1932-2023).

RAISING READERS
Books Build Bright Futures

Dear Reader,

We'd love your attention for one more page to tell you about the crisis in children's reading, and what we can all do.

Studies have shown that reading for fun is the **single biggest predictor of a child's future life chances** – more than family circumstance, parents' educational background or income. It improves academic results, mental health, wealth, communication skills, ambition and happiness.[1]

The number of children reading for fun is in rapid decline. Young people have a lot of competition for their time. In 2024, 1 in 10 children and young people in the UK aged 5 to 18 did not own a single book at home.[2]

Hachette works extensively with schools, libraries and literacy charities, but here are some ways we can all raise more readers:

- Reading to children for just 10 minutes a day makes a difference
- Don't give up if children aren't regular readers – there will be books for them!
- Visit bookshops and libraries to get recommendations
- Encourage them to listen to audiobooks
- Support school libraries
- Give books as gifts

There's a lot more information about how to encourage children to read on our website: **www.RaisingReaders.co.uk**

Thank you for reading.

---

[1] OECD, '21st-Century Readers: Developing Literacy Skills in a Digital World', 2021, https://www.oecd.org/en/publications/21st-century-readers_a83d84cb-en.html

[2] National Literacy Trust, 'Book Ownership in 2024', November 2024, https://literacytrust.org.uk/research-services/research-reports/book-ownership-in-2024